Ransom
Dunn

HILLSDALE'S GRAND OLD MAN

Ransom Dunn

ARLAN K. GILBERT

HILLSDALE COLLEGE PRESS
HILLSDALE, MICHIGAN

Hillsdale College Press

RANSOM DUNN
HILLSDALE'S GRAND OLD MAN
Arlan K. Gilbert

©2007 Hillsdale College Press, Hillsdale, Michigan 49242

First printing 2007

Printed in the United States of America

Front cover: Detail from *Ransom Dunn and Townsmen Envision Hillsdale College* by Sam Knecht. Courtesy Hillsdale College.

Cover design: Hesseltine & DeMason Design, Ann Arbor, Michigan

Library of Congress Control Number 2007923904

ISBN 978-0-916308-11-7

CONTENTS

PREFACE

America's Founders believed that education was vital to the preservation of freedom and self-government. Many of them had received the best formal or informal classical educations of their age.

Of the generations who followed the Founders, some who would prove the most indispensable to the survival of the Republic down to our own time were its leaders in education. Of these, Ransom Dunn, while not among the most famous, was among the greatest.

Dunn—for whom fame was not a motivation—established, financed, taught, and administered a college on the Western frontier beginning in the 1840s. This college was one of only 119 American colleges that granted four-year liberal arts degrees by 1850. It was also the first to prohibit by charter any discrimination based on race, sex, or religion. This was due to Dunn's influence, and to the fact that he and the other early leaders of Hillsdale were committed to America's founding principles.

By the 1870s, Hillsdale College was widely recognized as the finest small college in the West and one of the finest in the nation.

Dunn was connected with Hillsdale for nearly five decades, and it was here that his greatest and best work was accomplished. His association with the College continued until a few years before his death.

Dunn was motivated to provide the highest educational standards at the lowest cost for students who otherwise could not have attended college at all. The current president of Hillsdale College, Larry P. Arnn, describes Ransom Dunn as "probably the greatest man ever to work at our College."

As "Hillsdale's Grand Old Man," Dunn was insistent that graduates leave Hillsdale equipped not only with knowledge but with good character—ready not only to achieve professional success, but to provide moral leadership. The records of these graduates, more than anything else, established Hillsdale as an outstanding institution. Documentation of these records is available in my *Historic Hillsdale College: Pioneer in Higher Education, 1844–1900*; *Hillsdale Honor: The Civil War Experience*; and *The Permanent Things: Hillsdale College, 1900–1994*.

In this brief volume, I will show how Dunn's leadership was essential to the College's early survival and to its quickly gained prominence and influence. I will also show how his legacy still animates this sturdy liberal arts college that proudly defies the forces of progressivism, relativism, and governmental regulation of higher education. It is true that Dunn in his time—like his successors today—had a fine and dedicated supporting cast. But it is difficult to imagine how Hillsdale College could have overcome the obstacles it faced had it not been for the fortitude of this tall, physically frail but determined leader who gained strength by reading George Washington.

The *Hillsdale Leader* stated in his obituary: "The memory of Professor Dunn will long abide with Hillsdale people, a blessing, a benediction." Dunn's life was a blessing because it was animated by faith. And so may we find a blessing in learning about such a man. If in this book there is any lesson for future generations, it is because the subject was faithful. As Dunn said in an 1886 lecture, "Literature to be grand, to be interesting, must contain an underlying reference to God at heart. All the beauty of poetry depends upon it."* In the life of Dunn is found "an underlying reference to God at heart." Thus was his a poetic life.

★ ★ ★

I offer here some acknowledgments. For almost 40 years I had the high fortune of working with the College's Department of History, whose members believed and taught in accordance with moral principles largely ignored elsewhere during the wave of relativism that swept academia beginning in the 1960s.

Acknowledgments are also deserved by Eva Martin, Tracy Simmons, and Hans Zeiger. High praise is due the extraordinary editing of Doug Jeffrey, other editors of this biography, and to Jim Bowen who contributed his computer expertise.

As is fitting, this small volume is dedicated to the greater Hillsdale College community, each component of which is necessary to the continuing success of a staunch, God-fearing college. Thousands of people have contributed to the role of this Midwestern college that has been such a force for good in our country. My wife Gudrun and I are proud to have had a part in Hillsdale's continuing mission.

Dr. Arlan K. Gilbert
Hillsdale College Historian
Hillsdale, Michigan
December 2005

---

*Ransom Dunn, *Lectures in Theology* (Dover, NH: 1886).

Chapter One

YOUTH ON THE FRONTIER

★ ★ ★

LIKE MANY OTHER Americans in the new Republic, Ransom Dunn's ancestors had sailed for Massachusetts from London in the 1630s. One was taken prisoner in the French and Indian War; another died as a lieutenant in the battle at Saratoga in 1777.[1]

Ransom Dunn was born in a pioneer cabin at Bakersfield, Vermont, on July 7, 1818. One of ten children, his life was hard and stony like the New England soil. As a youth, he traveled by foot, stagecoach, and horseback. All three of his brothers became Christian preachers, and one would be appointed by General Benjamin Butler during the Civil War to be superintendent of schools for black children in New Orleans. All were influenced strongly by their self-educated father, who helped to establish a village library and served as a captain in the War of 1812. Dunn wrote that his father "never denied the existence of a God, the truth of the Bible, or the doctrine of immortality."[2]

Dunn attended the local Freewill Baptist Church, where the preacher was the Reverend William Arthur. Though Arthur's son

Chester was a decade Ransom's junior, the two played together. Both boys would become leaders in the nation; Chester A. Arthur would become president.[3]

Nobody would have predicted that Ransom Dunn would establish a college in the West. A sickly and sensitive boy, he spent many hours pursuing self-education by reading in front of the fireplace. He regularly walked three miles to a Sunday school library to obtain books, which formed the background for his becoming not only a successful pastor in Boston but also one of the nation's leading evangelists.

The first Freewill Baptist pastor to recognize the talents of young Ransom was Charles Bowles, a black native of Boston who ranged through Vermont preaching and organizing churches. Bowles admonished the young lad, who was four years old at the time, "My child, you must serve God."

Baptized in 1834, Ransom soon became aware of the religious needs of the new American West. "Conviction was upon me with awful force," he later recalled, "that it was my duty to go there and preach the Gospel."[4] Dunn's motivation also came from his reading of *Peck's Guide to Emigrants*. More important was the impact of *The Morning Star*, the official organ of the Freewill Baptists, which was launched in 1826 and published in Dover, New Hampshire. The publication of Charles Finney's revivalist views in his *Lectures on Revivals* in 1835 likewise stirred Dunn's missionary zeal.

However, the sensitive Dunn also had serious doubts about his calling. He wrote, "I knew my ability was inadequate, the means for an education impossible, inflammation of my eyes unfavorable for study."[5] Furthermore, his father's death in 1835 left Ransom with the responsibility of caring for his mother and the family farm.

In September 1836, eighteen-year-old Ransom Dunn was licensed to preach the Gospel by the monthly Freewill Baptist conference. He began his career by giving sermons in Vermont, New York, and Canada, but became convinced that his permanent calling was to the American West, beyond the Appalachians.

He was like the New Englanders of the time described by Alexis de Tocqueville in *Democracy in America*, "[abandoning] the land of their birth with the aim of going to lay the foundations of Christianity and freedom by the banks of the Mississippi or on the prairies of Illinois." Tocqueville saw both a religious and a political motive in these missionaries, a "religious zeal," he said, that

> constantly warms itself at the hearth of patriotism. You think that these men act solely in consideration of the other life, but you are mistaken: eternity is only one of their cares. If you interrogate these missionaries of Christian civilization, you will be altogether surprised to hear them speak so often of the goods of this world, and to find the political where you believe you will see only the religious. "All American republics are in solidarity with one another," they will say to you: "if the republics of the West fell into anarchy or came under the yoke of despotism, the republican institutions that flourish on the edges of the Atantic Ocean would be in great peril; we therefore have an interest in the new states" being religious so that they permit us to remain free.[6]

Leaving Vermont for Ohio in 1837, Ransom Dunn did not expect to see his family in the East again. To finance his Western ventures, the boy preacher supplemented the $13 he received from his father's estate with $8 in loans. He made his way to Ohio via the Erie Canal, and soon heard the words of the experienced minister J. B. Davis: "Religion is in a low state. We want men who have been called of God, willing to face cold storms, travel muddy roads, lodge in log houses—men who have the grace of God, and whose faces are set as a flint toward Zion. I believe God is calling some to come to Ohio."[7]

At the age of nineteen, Dunn began preaching at meetings in Ohio, and small collections enabled him to pay the debt for his trip from New England. The Freewill Baptist Quarterly Meeting in Tremble County, Ohio, ordained the young preacher on August 20, 1837. On one occasion Joshua Giddings and Ben Wade, then young lawyers in Ashtabula County, were greatly moved by one of Dunn's meetings. They recognized that Dunn was becoming a powerful evangelist.

Dunn usually hiked on his evangelistic preaching tours in Ohio. He held meetings in schoolhouses and private homes. Those who lived too far from the meeting houses often invited him to visit, pray, and eat with them.

Sometimes he lost his way in the drifting snows of the Midwestern winter. Even after obtaining a horse, Dunn faced such threats as mud, wolves, snowstorms, and lost paths. Several times he narrowly escaped death, and once he was thrown by his horse onto the frozen ground.

Dunn's fame as a preacher rapidly spread. At age 20, he became a major force in the great Ohio revivals in Tremble, Williamsfield, and Wayne counties. An observer wrote that after two hours of Dunn's preaching, "there was thunder and lightning, hail and earthquake."[8] During 1838 he led 365 meetings and traveled more than 3,000 miles. His audiences sometimes numbered more than 400. Throughout the Western Reserve, the powerful evangelist was eagerly sought by all denominations. Dr. George Ball, who founded Keuka College in upstate New York, described Dunn's oratory: "The young minister's preaching is like a tornado!"[9]

Dunn became so exhausted from preaching, travel, and lack of rest that he learned to sleep while riding horseback to his next meeting.

After three years of preaching on the frontier, Dunn returned to Vermont and New Hampshire to see his family in 1840. Going to Ohio several months later, he continued his acquaintance with Mary Eliza Allen, who was related to Revolutionary War hero Ethan Allen. Having known each other for two years, the young couple married that same year. Dunn's salary from preaching was only $200 a year, but their life was comfortable. Two sons were born to the Dunns in the early 1840s: Newell Ransom in 1841 and Francis Wayland two years later.

While in Ohio, Dunn began to enter the profession that was to occupy his life—that of teacher. Along with A. K. Moulton, he was appointed in 1844 by the Ohio and Pennsylvania Yearly Meeting to support the Geauga Academy at Chester, Ohio. It was here that he did his first theological teaching. Dunn rode more than 1,000 miles to promote the interests of the new school. It was during this period that he first demonstrated his strong antislavery feelings, as he successfully fought to change the original charter of the school from the Ohio legislature, which prohibited the admission of black students. Dunn's victory in this was significant, given that Ohio residents still held proslavery convictions. In 1853, the assets of this Free Will Baptist academy would be transferred to Hillsdale College.

Future president James A. Garfield was among the early students at the Geauga Academy. Dunn lectured at Geauga about the doctrine of atonement, but after Garfield's 1880 election the *Hillsdale Herald* would report that Dunn "confesses to the fact . . . that he didn't get [Garfield] quite sound on the baptism doctrine." Indeed,

Garfield became a member of the Disciples of Christ church.[10] Dunn then accepted the call to spend a year at a large Freewill Baptist Church in Dover, New Hampshire. This area was the center of the Freewill Baptist movement, and Dunn frequently lectured against slavery. The Freewill Baptists were second only to the Friends when it came to early religious antislavery prominence. As early as 1827, the Freewill Baptists' General Conference had authorized the ordination of blacks as ministers.[11] And in 1835 the General Conference declared slavery sinful.

In 1845 Dunn was elected president of the Antislavery Society, a powerful abolitionist group organized by the Freewill Baptists. That year he began to serve as pastor at the church in Great Falls, New Hampshire, a center of cotton manufacturing, where he continued his assault on slavery. By now Dunn had become one of the strongest antislavery leaders in New England. One of his parishioners in this period wrote, "To know him is to love him."

Still, Dunn's thoughts were of the West. He wrote, "God drove me West in my youth to work in that wide field independent of any society. And, God willing, that field I shall yet occupy. . . . The moment we fold our arms and cease to make aggressive movements, we die." He also wrote, "At the East I have fared well. . . . But I would not rest. A cry was in my ears from the West, and I am now on my way again to that field of labor. . . ."[12]

Dunn resisted the call of the West for only a year. The Geauga Academy and church at Chester needed him again. He was a member of the first Board of Trustees of the Academy, started in 1839 and chartered in 1840. Dunn felt obliged to accept the call.

In his farewell, a speech of commitment to the West, he concluded, "Something must be done now. Unless we awake and go into this great Western field the harvest will perish, souls be lost, God dishonored, and we condemned. . . ."[13] Among those who heard Dunn's speech was Edmund B. Fairfield, an alumnus of Oberlin College. These two men were to meet again, as they undertook the arduous task of founding Hillsdale College on the frontier of southern Michigan. An observer of Dunn's impassioned farewell statement commented, "Hardship, unending toil, and scanty remuneration were the reward of him who cast his lot with the West."[14]

Dunn now confronted the first of many personal sorrows that were to fill his life. In 1848, his wife, Mary Eliza Dunn, suffered from a worsening case of consumption. In hopes of helping her recover, the family moved back to Ohio in May, but the climate helped little. She died on August 4, 1848.

Hoping to offer his family some relief, Dunn planned a trip farther West. With his two young sons and a daughter (Cedelia, born in 1845), he traveled by steamboat down the Ohio River, and then south on the Mississippi. In St. Louis Dunn preached in a black church, his first opportunity to speak to slaves. Then the family proceeded north to Galena, Illinois, before returning to Cleveland, Ohio. The trip, an extensive one for the time, helped to prepare Dunn for his later tasks in raising endowment for Hillsdale College.

Returning to the East in June 1849, Dunn temporarily accepted pastoral duties in New York City and then in Boston. He accepted the latter position in spite of poor health and low finances: "The afflictions of the past year have taken all of my earthly goods . . . but, hoping for the best, it is my design to 'spend and be spent' for the cause of Christ."[15]

Dunn's spirits were improved by his marriage in September 1849 to Cyrena Emery in Dover, New Hampshire. Cyrena was descended from officers who had fought in the American Revolution. One of her ancestors, Noah Emery, gave the property to found

Dartmouth College in 1769 and wrote the official copy of the Declaration of Independence for the state house at Concord, New Hampshire.

While directing his church in Boston, Dunn wrote articles for *The Christian Observer* and other newspapers. On March 1, 1850, Dunn delivered to his congregation what would be the most famous sermon of his career. Published thereafter by the Boston Quarterly Meeting, Dunn's "Discourse on the Freedom of the Will" continues to be read by students of theology and American religious history today. In this sermon, Dunn refuted Jonathan Edwards and other Calvinists who argued for predestination; Dunn believed that God had given to mankind the freedom of choice. God knows all things, he believed, but God does not manipulate all actions.

> God's foreknowledge, then, although it makes it certain that an event does occur, no more makes it certain that such an event might not have been otherwise, than my knowledge of your presence here today makes it certain that you could not have been elsewhere. You could have been elsewhere, and then the knowledge of your position would have been accordingly. Our actions might have been different from what they are, and God's knowledge would have been according to the facts in the case. The idea that simple knowledge implies necessity with respect to cause, is not according to sound philosophy, common sense, nor the Bible.[16]

Furthermore, he argued, human responsibility could not be accounted for other than by moral independence. Language, law, and conscience pointed to man's accountability for his own actions, thoughts, and decisions.

Upon the supposition of its truth, man at once appears an accountable being; he himself, and no other one, being responsible for his volitions. He is thus rendered a fit subject of moral government. The institution of human governments, and the organization of the family, with all the voluntary relations and influences growing out of them, are thus made legitimate and reasonable. Language and the most plain decisions of consciousness, which would otherwise present the most inexplicable difficulties, are thus rendered plain and simple. The atonement, with all the means of grace, the disciplinary influences of providence, and all human efforts for the change of character, which would otherwise be but a solemn farce, at once appear necessary and consistent.[17]

Reason, Dunn thought, was as necessary as Scripture to completing a proper idea of the will, or to any other topic for that matter. The "Bible is not given for a scientific text book," Dunn said, "nor for a system of philosophy. Those natural common matters of fact with which we are able to become acquainted by other means, are there taken for granted."[18] Dunn believed that the Bible was consistent with reason, and that reason was among the gifts God had given to man to accommodate his freedom of choice. Thus learning was the cultivation of liberty.

During his two-year pastorate in Boston, Dunn became an interested spectator at surgical operations in Massachusetts General Hospital. He also attended lectures on anatomy and physiology by Oliver Wendell Holmes and others at Harvard University. He recorded that his study of natural theology for more than a decade led him to this natural interest in medicine.

Dunn's pastoral activity was temporarily interrupted by a serious accident while returning in a carriage from a baptism in Boston. His driver carelessly flicked his whip, breaking Dunn's spectacles and driving fragments of glass into his eye. Dunn's sight was endangered. The best physicians in Boston saved the inflamed eye, but the experience and treatments weakened his already frail body. He never regained the twenty pounds he lost during this period, and eyestrain would plague him for the rest of his long life.

In February 1851 his physicians in Boston informed him that rest was the only remedy for his weakness. His years of preaching had taken their toll, and Dunn wrote that for the moment he was "a rambling, itinerant lecturer. . . . The flower and vigor of [his life having] been spent in the ministry and without accumulating anything."[19] Dunn considered giving a series of popular talks on his newfound study of medicine in the event he could not continue preaching.

Instead, he once again decided to go West, leaving in April of that year. Traveling mainly by barge and steamboat, he and his family reached Wisconsin in May. Weak but determined, Dunn made lecturing tours in Wisconsin, Ohio, Illinois, and Iowa. His family settled in a rough farmhouse on the prairie east of Galena. A second daughter, Cyrena, was born there, but her health was frail. The family grew lonely and restless. Then, an unexpected call to a new field of labor came to Ransom Dunn. His most challenging lifework was about to begin.

★ ★ ★

Chapter Two

A HIGH CALLING

✷ ✷ ✷

T HE FREEWILL BAPTIST denomination originated in New England in the late eighteenth century as a reaction against the prevailing Calvinism. It dated from 1780, when the Baptist Church in New Hampshire ejected Elder Benjamin Randall "on account of his belief in free will and in a free and full salvation."[20] By 1830 there were an estimated 400 Freewill Baptist churches in the country, with a total membership of 16,000. The church's membership peaked in 1900, with almost 90,000 adherents. In 1911 it formally merged with the American (Northern) Baptist Convention in a conference at a Michigan college whose history had commenced 77 years prior.[21]

It was in June of 1844 that the Freewill Baptist Michigan Yearly Meeting addressed the question of Christian higher education within its boundary. The membership decided to locate an institution at Spring Arbor, Michigan. This step was unusual because the Baptists in America did not inherit from Europe a tradition of an educated ministry. Indeed, an active prejudice against the education of ministers was evident.[22] Another handicap to be overcome was that many of the fewer than 1,000 Freewill Baptists in Michigan lived in poverty, in debt trying to pay for their land.[23] Despite these circumstances, the Freewill Baptists brought about the establishment of a permanent and prominent institution, Hillsdale College in Michigan.

By December 1844, Oberlin College graduate D. M. Graham began teaching at the small school (originally called Michigan Central College), which was located in an old storefront near an Indian burial ground. The initial enrollment of six students increased to 25 by July 1845. By the following winter, a college building was constructed and enrollment reached 70. Work proceeded on the construction of a second building.

The idea behind the institution was unique. Based from the beginning on the principle of nondiscrimination, the school admitted females and blacks on equal footing with males and whites. Faith underlaid the enterprise. The College would later adopt a Freewill Baptist Church Covenant that included the following: "We will everywhere hold Christian principles sacred and Christian obligations and enterprises supreme; counting it our chief business in life to extend the influence of Christ in society; constantly praying and toiling that the Kingdom of God may come, and his will be done on earth as it is in heaven."[24]

The college held its first graduation exercises in June 1848. The educational examiner from the state of Michigan listened to twelve ladies and nineteen men give declamations. He reported that the students "showed originality of thought and manliness of learning found only in institutions of the West." The examiner also visited fifteen classes in mathematics, Latin, Greek, and English. A total of 126 students had attended during the year.

Edmund B. Fairfield, who earlier had heard Dunn speak, came from Oberlin College to serve as president and teach at Michigan Central College in October 1848. Immediately he set out to recruit Ransom Dunn to teach at the college. "The Institution here, I find is but in its infancy," Fairfield wrote to Dunn on November 20. "But in many respects the prospect is highly favorable. . . . My object in writing to you at present is to inquire whether you could so arrange your affairs as to engage with us in this work. We want you; we need you."[25] Two days later, Fairfield wrote again, repeating his plea: "We must make this Institution live. It can live and thrive, and accomplish much for our Denomination."[26]

Indeed, signs of growth were on the horizon. The school had a library of 1,500 volumes. The official state policy of Michigan had been to grant no charter with college privileges except to the University of Michigan. But Michigan Central College, soon to become Hillsdale College, successfully obtained a charter because of supporters in the state legislature. By 1851, this first chartered college in Michigan, and the first to admit women and blacks, was ready for greater work. Tuition was $6 a term and board was $1 a week. More applicants sought admission than could be accepted. (Per capita expenses at the University of Michigan at this time were between $70 and $100 per annum.) The staggering problem was the lack of finances for professors, buildings, and equipment. If the college was truly to thrive, Ransom Dunn's help would be needed. Fairfield again wrote to Dunn on December 22, 1851, inviting him to lead the school to a stronger future. "Make no other calculations but to be here as early as may be," he wrote.[27] Fairfield offered Dunn an appointment as Professor of Mental and Moral Philosophy and Political Economy. Although he had never seen the College, Dunn accepted the call and immediately traveled to Spring Arbor in a carriage with his wife and baby Cyrena. Following in a wagon were his three older children and the family's possessions. Through snow and intense cold they drove past Chicago and boarded a train at Michigan City.

Upon arrival at Spring Arbor in January 1852, Dunn began teaching five classes daily, correcting student essays, and hearing declamations. He also handled all student accounts. Among Dunn's students was Livonia E. Benedict, the first woman to receive a classical degree in Michigan. In addition, Dunn continued to hold revival meetings, and crowds flocked from miles around to hear him preach.

Thus Dunn began the work that was to consume his energy for the rest of his life, almost half a century. Meanwhile, Mrs. Dunn took charge of the boarding hall with twenty students.

A minister visiting the school in June wrote: "Recitation rooms are small, laboratory in a little room . . . but the institution stands well at home and abroad. . . . The well known energy and popularity of Brothers Fairfield and Dunn peculiarly fit them for securing the confidence and sympathy of the people."[28]

Dunn became convinced soon after his arrival at Spring Arbor that the college could not be successful in that location. In this small town away from any railroads and without people of sufficient means to support the institution, a college of the quality Dunn desired could not be built. A third building was needed immediately, but the community lacked interest.

Endorsed by a few other new professors, Dunn became leader of the movement to relocate the College.[29] The meeting of the Board of Trustees on January 5, 1853—a "stormy session"—resulted in a 9 to 2 vote to consider the expediency of moving the College to a more suitable location. On January 19, the Board appointed a committee to confer with citizens of the Michigan towns of Jackson, Coldwater, Adrian, Marshall, and Hillsdale.[30]

Delayed by a snowstorm on the way to Coldwater, Professor Dunn decided to head alone on horseback to Hillsdale, a village of about 2,000. There he arranged for a conference with leading citizens. The evening meeting was attended by twenty men—judges, bankers, professionals, and businessmen—and not one was a Freewill Baptist. Dunn had expected only four or five men to show such interest. His forty-minute speech settled "the fate and fortune of Hillsdale College, and changed the destiny of thousands for all time."[31] Dunn specified that the College was to be denominational but not narrowly sectarian. It should furnish no special advantages to any denomination, nor should it make distinctions based on sex or color. As one historian later wrote, "Hillsdale had captured the professor, and the professor had captured Hillsdale."[32]

At the meeting with Dunn, it was agreed that the Hillsdale community leaders should help to construct the college buildings, while the Freewill Baptists raised the endowment. The next morning three men showed Dunn suitable sites for the undertaking. Wading through mud, crossing a swamp to a half-cleared pasture with a split-rail fence, they reached the final location, now College Hill. Deer, partridge, turkey, and quail were numerous. Dunn stepped up onto a large stump (close to present-day Central Hall) and proclaimed, "If ever we have a Freewill Baptist college in the West, it will be within four rods of this stump."[33]

Fairfield, meanwhile, had been favorably impressed by Coldwater. Although the committee from Michigan Central College had recommended Coldwater as the best location to the trustees on January 19, 1853, Dunn insisted that Hillsdale was more desirable and could raise more funds. Furthermore, the completion in 1843 of what became the Michigan Southern Railroad, which connected Hillsdale with Toledo, had already brought prosperity to the young town.[34] The Michigan Southern was the first railroad to provide complete rail connections between Chicago and the cities of the eastern seaboard.[35] Hillsdale would be at this time the only town in the United States that already had railroad facilities prior to selection as a Baptist college site.[36]

Fairfield was persuaded. On January 26, he wrote to Dunn that the people of Coldwater were supportive of the college, "But at H there is a regular furor. That will be our destination; and I am glad of it. They are whole-hearted in the movement."[37]

The citizens of Spring Arbor were angered at the idea of losing "their" College, and some residents held a meeting protesting the move. They passed a resolution on January 29 describing "Professors Fairfield, Dunn, Churchill, and Thompson as unworthy of their confidence and support."[38] In less than a month, however, the committee of location met at Dunn's home and decided to relocate to Hillsdale. An amount of $20,000 was pledged in Hillsdale County if an additional $17,000 could be raised elsewhere. Twenty-five acres of land were provided for the campus. Construction of the buildings began in the summer of 1853.

On July 6, the trustees voted to "appoint Ransom Dunn agent, with full power of attorney, to take such measures as he may deem expedient to raise funds."[39] Specifically, he was assigned the task of raising an endowment of $10,000 in Illinois, Wisconsin, Iowa, and Minnesota. This area was almost without transportation facilities, and the churches had very few members, most of them poor. Dunn responded: "It had seemed to me worse than death to commence preaching, but to undertake this agency seemed still worse. But after weeping the first ten miles the work was prosecuted with what energy I could command."[40] Dunn realized that a long campaign was needed for him to secure $10,000 from the scattered Freewill Baptists west of Lake Michigan. He moved his family to Wisconsin, which would allow him to see them occasionally.

The Bentley Historical Library at the University of Michigan contains the "First subscription list for Hillsdale College, Made by Dr. Dunn, from Sept. 1853 to opening of school in 1855." This lists the sources of the first endowment of Hillsdale College. Most of the money came in small gifts from people living in log houses, shanties, and other humble dwellings with few necessities. The infant college was the beneficiary of donations from poor men, farmers with mortgages on their land, and ministers living on $200 or $300 a year. Overworking his frail body in the middle of a cholera epidemic, Dunn's achievements reached heroic proportions. He would not rest until his task had been completed. In two years, Dunn raised $22,000, more than twice the original goal of $10,000.[41]

Not only did Dunn secure an endowment, he also obtained funds for students to attend Hillsdale College, raising money for a scholarship plan. A contribution of $100 provided the donor with permanently free tuition for one student at a time. Many young people were able to attend college because of these donations. The endowment Dunn raised allowed Hillsdale College to charge such low tuition that poor but ambitious students could obtain a higher education.

Dunn protected the funds that he had raised by influencing the trustees to pass the following resolution: "Resolved, that the principal of all funds raised toward the endowment of the College by donations or the sale of scholarships outside of Hillsdale County shall be held forever sacred, the interest only to be expended."[42] In addition to raising endowments and selling scholarships, Dunn, by the force of his appeals, attracted students to Hillsdale. O. A. Janes was one of many young men drawn to Hillsdale after hearing Dunn speak on his Western tour. He later wrote to Dunn, "I well remember you, when I was a boy, at Johnston, Wisconsin, pleading for Hillsdale College and preaching in the old stone schoolhouse.

I then made up my mind that I should attend college at Hillsdale. In later years. . . . I knew of your zeal on raising money for the college, and to you more than to any one else is due its success."[43]

As if his onerous tasks on the frontier were not enough, Dunn also helped to organize churches in Wisconsin and Illinois. In all, he dedicated five churches during his Western trip.

And Dunn's work in raising endowment for Hillsdale was far from over.

His efforts were gaining recognition. That he championed the new college in the West caused the Freewill Baptist General Conference in 1854 to pass a resolution to raise $25,000 for Hillsdale College.

Without doubt, Dunn was the primary influence on the relocation of the College from Spring Arbor. One Hillsdale supporter, the Honorable C. C. Mitchell, a lumberman, later wrote, "I have always regarded you as the principal founder of Hillsdale College and its most steadfast friend, and as having raised more money than anyone else for its endowment. And while I was a trustee your influence was always for the safe management of its finances."

★ ★ ★

Chapter Three

THE EMERGENCE OF
HILLSDALE COLLEGE

★ ★ ★

WHILE DUNN WAS RAISING endowment in the West, construction of the relocated college began. Esbon Blackmar had contributed 25 acres—which form today's campus quadrangle —and a building committee, including Dunn, was at work. On June 7, 1853, Edmund Fairfield wrote to Dunn: "We have contracted for 1,000,000 brick. The buildings are to be enclosed this fall. . . . All moves right."[44] On July 4, the college cornerstone was laid in the presence of the largest group of people ever convened in Hillsdale. Dunn, in unusually high spirits, offered the prayer of consecration. The youthful poet Will Carleton was among those in the large crowd who were much impressed by the words of the tall, pale man with high forehead.[45] The last commencement at Michigan Central in Spring Arbor took place two days later, on July 6, 1853.

By August, the cellars were dug and foundations laid. But legal difficulties delayed further progress during 1854 because citizens from Spring Arbor had placed an injunction on the trustees to prevent the relocation of the College. The issue was settled in favor of Hillsdale. Another matter was to remove any doubts about the legality of the college charter. Fortunately, the Michigan Senate and House were led by Hillsdale supporters, and a bill was passed in February of 1855 that recognized the right of Hillsdale to confer degrees. All private Michigan colleges owe their right to grant degrees to these successful efforts of Hillsdale.

In accordance with the legal charter, 35 trustees were elected for the College; their first annual meeting was held in July 1855. As one of the original trustees, Ransom Dunn would be present at 38 of the 43 meetings held between 1855 until his death in 1900; he was absent only when ill health prevented his involvement, and, in later years, when faculty members were not allowed to serve as trustees.

When the first college faculty was elected, Ransom Dunn received the most votes. In accordance with Dunn's resolution, only the interest—not the principal—of the endowment could be spent, so faculty salaries ranged from $400 to $700. Operating within the college's means continued to be the policy of the trustees.

Hillsdale College officially opened in November 1855. Its earliest years illustrated the Emersonian combination of "plain living and high thinking." From the beginning, Professor Dunn proclaimed the principle of equal rights of all persons without regard to color or sex. Politically, Hillsdale County in the early 1850s was strongly Democratic and opposed abolitionism. But Ransom Dunn and Edmund Fairfield influenced the county to support the Free Soilers, and the county soon became a leading force in the new Republican ranks of Michigan. A student who later fought in the Civil War offered this toast to Dunn: "To you who so efficiently helped to plant in the oak openings of Michigan an abolition college which has blest and helped thousands—that is glory enough for one man."[46]

Unfortunately, the man who had done more than anyone to bring the College into existence had to miss the official opening because of eye inflammation. He was under a physician's care in Boston for a year, and only after 18 months was his sight restored. Another sorrow arose in October of 1855, when the Dunns' four-year-old daughter Cyrena died from typhoid fever. Dunn lamented, "A sweeter spirit never rejoiced a parent's heart. She was the idol of the family. But she has gone to a better clime. It is all right. God knows best."[47]

By the fall of 1857 Dunn was able to return to his duties at Hillsdale. (His name had been kept in the college catalogue throughout his absence.) He had rejected a handsome offer of $100 in gold each month to remain at the large Bennett Street Church in Boston where he had achieved much success. The small College on the frontier was his priority, although Dunn admitted that "my departure from Boston at this time was one of the most painful separations of my life."[48] One of Dunn's contributions to Hills-dale's growth was the acquisition of Geauga Academy. Attendance at Geauga by 1848–49 had reached 252 students. The academy offered not only a basic classical education, but also an introduction to respectable living.[49] As early as May 1853, the Hillsdale trustees appointed Dunn as correspondent with the Geauga Academy "with reference to securing with them a community of interest." The two institutions soon joined.

In Dunn's absence, professors and students had successfully met the challenges of their new college on the frontier. By 1858, the trustees had granted halls to Hillsdale's strong literary societies. Dunn delivered an address titled "Antagonism of Mind with Mind" for the Amphictyons' room on August 18, 1858; the hall had satin cloth lining the walls and a Brussels carpet. He also dedicated the Alphas' new hall with a speech titled "True Greatness" on July 29, 1859.

When the Dunn family returned to the College in 1857, they had taken rooms in the college boarding hall. Dunn's teaching salary of $600 was increased to $900 because he also regularly preached for the students. Indeed, one of his strongest influences upon the College was through his preaching in the chapel. When Judge Richmond Melendy, a hero of the Civil War, returned to his alma mater years later and addressed chapel, he related the story of a young student who claimed to dislike sitting under Dunn's preaching on hot days. Asked the reason, he replied, "Because I forget to fan myself while he is talking."[50]

Dunn's two sons already were taking courses in the college. Cedelia, thirteen years of age, was ready to begin her studies, but in May of 1858 she died from scarlet fever. This first death in the college building made a deep impression on the students. Now Dunn's first wife and two daughters were in their graves. In addition, the nation was in crisis and one of his two sons would soon make the ultimate sacrifice in the Union army. Only a father's heart could know such agony.

On September 24, 1858, students showed their respect for Professor Dunn by giving him a surprise party, complete with brass band, which remained silent until reaching Dunn's home. He invited all the marchers in, and the students gave him a purse containing $150.[51]

At this time Dunn agreed once again to accept a position in Boston, this time at the influential Tremont Temple Church. But his fragile constitution again caused him to leave his duties as minister, and in 1861 he took a trip to the nation's capital. He carried letters of introduction to prominent congressmen, senators, and other well-known politicians in Washington, many of whom became strong supporters of Hillsdale College.

To regain his health, Dunn moved his family to a farm near Ottawa, Illinois. Here he lost a third child, when two-year-old Lily passed away. Brother Wayland wrote, "Another sister gone." Fortunately Dunn's health gradually improved with the activity of plowing, planting, and building a home. Although busy in farm work, he continued to preach frequently on the frontier. A listener reported, "He is certainly one among a thousand, the best speaker I ever heard."[52] Meanwhile, the work of building the new college in Hillsdale had just begun.

★ ★ ★

Chapter Four

HILLSDALE AND THE UNION

★ ★ ★

RANSOM DUNN, a longtime antislavery activist, was well aware of the approaching national crisis during his pastorate in Boston. In a Memorial Day speech years later, he noted that the denomination, although small, played an important part in shaping public opinion during this period.[53]

On his two-year Western trip raising Hillsdale's initial endowment, Dunn had taken time to speak out against slavery. In 1853, he spoke eloquently at the Freewill Baptist General Conference at Fairport, New York. One of his listeners later wrote, "Yours was the grand pioneer declaration [on antislavery] toward which the nation soon began to drift. But this was before the days of the Republican party, which you prophesied would be formed. . . . It is not strange that when I learned of Hillsdale College and that you were to be one of the faculty I determined to go to this Christian and antislavery college."[54]

The antislavery position of Hillsdale College was one of the strongest in the nation. Such early students as Clinton B. Fisk, who became a general in the Civil War, were avowed abolitionists. Fisk wrote to President Lincoln on October 24, 1863: "I believe Slavery to be the cause and strength of the rebellion, and I desire that Slavery should die."[55] Daniel McBride Graham, first president of Michigan Central College, had been a leader serving on the executive committee of the American and Foreign Anti-Slavery Society from 1853 to 1855.

It was only natural, then, that Hillsdale's male student body enlisted and left for war after the attack on Fort Sumter in 1861. By the end of the Civil War, at least 420 Hillsdale students had enlisted in the Union army. The college's president and professors often left their classes to make political speeches, and students drilled on the college quad.[56]

Ransom Dunn requested only that his two sons graduate from college before enlisting. They were still quite young and would have time for military service if the conflict lasted a year. Meantime they had the opportunity to hear prominent abolitionist Owen Lovejoy speak on the battle of Bull Run. When the two Dunn boys graduated on June 19, 1862, Newell Ransom was 21 years of age, and Francis Wayland was 19. They enlisted in the Yates Sharpshooters, the Sixty-Fourth Regiment of the Illinois Volunteers. Their father expressed a wish that he could enlist with them and join the war effort.

In September the Dunn brothers began their march south, where they were stationed at Corinth, Mississippi. Newell wrote to his father that the Yankee soldiers there were "a hard set of boys, hard set every way, drinking brandy, sipping whiskey . . . they all play cards and drink when they get a chance."[57] Hillsdale College men frequently made such complaints about the behavior of fellow troops. Wayland wrote to his father on February 27, 1863, that "a man sees so much that is rough and wicked in camp that he soon finds himself looking on with indifference, but after all I believe I shall come out all right. . . ."[58] Wayland also complained about the number of political generals: "All of the field officers are political wire pullers, policy men who have got their positions through favor and not because they were fitted for them."[59]

Dunn's sons also wrote to him of meeting and hearing from former Hillsdale students who remembered their father's outstanding teaching. Sometimes these students would write to Dunn directly. Joseph McKnight, Captain of the Fifth Wisconsin Battery, wrote that "the Emancipation Proclamation was the climax of the development of a settled policy, alike beneficial to the government and humanity."[60] Both Dunn brothers lamented that "it is a matter of curiosity to see the intense prejudice [of northern troops] against the blacks. . . . This is the only thing that you will find urged in all talk among the soldiers."[61] Wayland contemplated gathering fifty or sixty black refugees hiding in the swamps and bringing them out to freedom.

Ransom and Wayland spent free time reading the Bible, the *Iliad*, and *Ivanhoe*. Unfortunately, they had no chaplain in their regiment, and Wayland wrote that he had not heard a sermon since he enlisted. The brothers passed unhurt through several battles. But in March 1863, Ransom was taken sick with typhoid fever caused by poor water and exposure from serving extra time on guard for a sick friend. Wayland helped him to the regimental hospital and procured some pure water, milk, and eggs. For several weeks, Ransom's health continued to fail, and he was given communion. Wayland wrote home to his father: "Before this time the telegraph has informed you of the saddest news that I can ever write. . . . He died Thursday morning about 6 o'clock. I was with him from one in the night until that time. . . . The doctor came in and gave him some stimulant and put a poultice on his breast. . . . But just at sunrise I noticed a sudden change in his countenance. . . . I knew it was his last and gave him some stimulant. . . . He could only drink two or three swallows and then I asked him, 'Is it all right, Ransom?' He turned his eyes upward and kept them so until they were clouded over."[62]

The next morning Wayland had the corpse sealed in a wooden coffin for the eventual memorial service in Hillsdale. Wayland wrote to his father that on the day before he died, his brother asked to have a piece of bread and to take communion with the phrase, "Do this in remembrance of me." He ended this letter: "Now father let us be resigned and trust in that source of all comfort."[63]

Wayland then had to face the almost impossible task of getting his brother's corpse home. Trains were allowed to carry only military cargoes. When he finally succeeded, his father's acknowledgment of its arrival was stoic, "The corpse arrived all safe this evening and I have telegraphed for Pres. Fairfield or Prof. Whipple to preach the sermon next Sabbath. . . .[64]

Ransom Dunn laid to rest his namesake in Oak Grove Cemetery north of campus. Every Decoration Day, beginning in 1868, Hillsdale's faculty and student body proceeded solemnly up West Street to place flowers on the graves of Newell Ransom Dunn and others of his classmates who gave their lives in the war. Above the cemetery entrance for many years arched a sign: "The Army of Our Dead."[65]

Now Professor Dunn observed that it was almost impossible for him to write or study, as he was burdened by one of the saddest trials of his life. He had done all he could to aid his two sons and to help them obtain an education. But now one lay dead, and the other still served in the army. Four of his children had passed away. And news soon arrived that his brother Thomas had died in New

Orleans. A chaplain in the army, Thomas Dunn had been called "the good angel of the colored people."[66]

In 1862, Dunn assumed a new responsibility at Hillsdale College—head of the Theological Department and professor of theology. He spent much time writing letters to former students in the field. In return, Lt. Jacob H. Stark wrote: "Believe me [that I am] sincerely anxious to become a Christian. I may be doomed to fall in the closing struggle, and should I, I wish to fall close to the stars and stripes and clinging to the cross of Christ."[67] Chaplain N. Woodworth of the 31st Wisconsin wrote to Dunn from Atlanta about helping the freedmen: "I hope the Freedmen's Aid Society that makes Hillsdale a center, will make this place a field of labor just as soon as possible. . . . I have had charge of a church and colored congregations since we came to this place."[68]

On July 7, 1864, Dunn was notified by Michigan Governor Austin Blair that he had been appointed military agent for Michigan under the U.S. Sanitary Commission formed on February 18, 1863. His specific duty was to evaluate sanitary conditions of the Michigan troops at the front and to promote the relief of sick, disabled, and needy soldiers. Dunn visited the troops of the Army of the Cumberland and also in the Kenesaw Mountain area, where he met with his son Wayland.[69] He carried papers addressed to the Provost Marshall General in Chattanooga: "This will introduce Professor Dunn of Hillsdale College, Michigan, who is commissioned by Governor Blair as agent for the purpose of visiting and ascertaining the sanitary condition of the Michigan troops at the front."[70] Dunn would have liked to participate more directly in the war, but he followed the advice of a friend: "I think you can do more good to stay at home and give your influence to aid on the work of emancipation by 'speechifying.'"[71]

In his last year of military service, Wayland Dunn was Second Lieutenant in the First U.S. Cavalry, Alabama Volunteers, part of Sherman's army. He wrote of scouting Georgia locations including Dallas, Resaca, Kenesaw Mountain, Marietta, Rome, Big Shanty, and Atlanta. In the fall of 1864, Wayland was mustered out of the army and returned home. Looking to his future, he commented, "I have no plans at least none that assume any tangible shape just as McCormick had no tangible prospects about his reaper until he had tried it and found the thing would cut."[72]

Upon hearing his father preach again, Wayland wrote, "There is no better speaker in the United States than this father of mine. Sometimes in fervent and impassioned passages I almost fear he can't keep it up and will fail, but failure is not in his book."[73]

✳ ✳ ✳

Chapter Five

POSTWAR PROGRESS

★ ★ ★

IN THE FALL OF 1865 Professor Dunn and his son took an extensive trip through much of Europe and the Middle East. This venture, which included Great Britain, Scotland, Ireland, France, Italy, Egypt, Palestine, Switzerland, and Germany, was financed by a gift of $1,000 from friends. The journey lasted eight months and, in the future, provided a constant source of conversation with his friends and students.

Upon returning to Hillsdale, Dunn again took up the double burden of professor and pastor. Soon after his return, a factional issue occurred on the Hillsdale campus. The cause of the controversy was a faculty order that persons of the opposite sex could not be admitted to any literary society meeting without first presenting a pass signed by the College president. To this point, the literary societies at the College not only flourished, but were also probably the most popular element of campus life. They featured nationally prominent guest lecturers, student debates, musical performances, and student oratory. The change caused by the faculty order was a radical one, because from the societies' beginning regular meetings had been open to the public. The societies refused to obey, and the faculty was equally adamant. What resulted was a general strike of the male student body. Large numbers of students were expelled, and the societies were abandoned for almost a year.

Dunn came to the rescue in this controversy, as he openly defied President Fairfield. In 1864, he had formed a fifth literary society, the Theological Association. He therefore had a vested interest in the dispute, and he persuaded the faculty to give him a list of ladies he could invite to the Theological Association meetings without the President's countersignature. Fairfield proceeded to give the same privilege of inviting women to the other four societies. The departed students were pardoned and allowed to return and the "Great Rebellion" was at an end.

H. M. Ford, one of Dunn's students, compared the preaching of Dunn and Fairfield: "They were so different they could hardly be compared. Dunn was chain lightning, a cyclone, a torrent carrying all before him. His oratory at times was awe-inspiring, like standing before Niagara. Fairfield was like a modern four hundred ton locomotive sweeping majestically along without much noise and every part synchronized."[74] Different in style and sometimes in ideas though these two founders of Hillsdale College were, together they made the place "live," as Fairfield had described his goal to Dunn in 1848.

Dunn served as pastor of Hillsdale's Freewill Baptist Church from 1857 to 1859, 1863 to 1870, and 1879 to 1883. "Each Sunday Professor Dunn would by his fevered oratory take us up to the walls of the New Jerusalem, where we gazed on the streets paved with gold," L. N. Keating later recalled.[75] The church had originally met in the chapel on campus, but following the Civil War, Dunn oversaw the construction of a church large enough for commencement and other college functions. He raised every subscription for this undertaking but one, for a total of $20,000. In January of 1868, the building—which became known as College Baptist Church—was dedicated. Dunn based his sermon on Genesis 28:"Surely the Lord is in this place. . . . This is none other but the house of God, and this is the gate of heaven."

Another of Dunn's enterprises was the establishment of a Western denominational publication, *The Christian Freeman*, published in Chicago. His son Wayland became editor. Unfortunately, Wayland's health, already weakened by his wartime service, began to break under the pressures of editorial work for this project. In the summer of 1868, Mrs. Dunn's health also began to fail.

While his wife was in Chicago for medical treatment, Dunn was proposed as a candidate for the United States Congress. He declined the nomination because of his work in Hillsdale. After residing for a brief time in Nebraska to allow his wife and son to regain their health, Dunn rejected the call of a large Chicago church in 1871 and returned to Hillsdale to accept the most important call of his life. President Fairfield had resigned, and it was imperative that Dunn take over the leadership of the College.

Hillsdale College had by this time gained wide recognition. A Lansing newspaper reported that Hillsdale, with the exception of the State University, stood at the head of all institutions of learning in Michigan, both in point of numbers and thoroughness of instruction. "Among its Faculty have been found in years past, as we also find at this time, some of the ripest scholars of the age."[76] Another newspaper reported that Hillsdale ranked among the best educational institutions in the nation. Many of Hillsdale's students and graduates went to the South to teach the freedmen. Among institutions that encouraged their alumni to become educational agents in the former Confederacy, Hillsdale was one of the strongest.

In the life of a college, the time had been brief. In the life of a man, it had been long. Ransom Dunn already was the "dean" of the faculty in length of service. In 1873 his hard work was recognized with an honorary doctorate from Bates College.

Unfortunately, his son Wayland did not recover his health. He accepted the chair of belles lettres at Hillsdale, but it was only a matter of months until his brief professorship would end. An outstanding young professor, Wayland developed tuberculosis and endured intense pain preceding his death on December 13, 1874.

His life being attended by so many trials, Dunn's accomplishments appear all the more remarkable. His own health often suffered from the strain. In 1870, the *Hillsdale Standard* reported the hope that Dr. Dunn's health would be such as to enable him to take the professorship in the Theological Department. It was characteristic of the Dunns' continuing compassion for others that the family had cared for senior student George A. Slayton in their home when he became ill. Slayton and his wife would later give the land for a beautiful arboretum to the College.

Another catastrophe for the College and for Ransom Dunn occurred in 1874. On March 6, during spring vacation, a fire broke out in West Hall. Dunn directed the battle against the fire, but both West Hall and the central building were demolished; only East Hall was left standing. Students tried to rescue the furniture of their society halls, and soaked carpets were placed on the roof of East Hall to discourage the flames. Students climbed the dome of the central building carrying buckets of water, but were driven down by the fire and smoke. The next day, the campus was in ruins.

The Board of Trustees met immediately "to consider measures for the rebuilding of the College structures which were destroyed by fire this morning."[77] The faculty began holding classes in the church, private houses offered rooms to students, and plans were made to

rebuild. The work of the College went on without significant inter-
ruption. When the cornerstone for a new building was laid in August
1874, Ransom Dunn delivered a magnificent speech on the "History and Mission of the College." He also offered the consecrating
prayer, the same service he had performed at the cornerstone-laying
ceremony more than twenty-one years earlier.[78]

Dunn took a leave of absence during the rebuilding of the
campus, answering the call to direct the establishment of Rio
Grande College in Jackson, Ohio, to which he commuted for three
years. He was known at Rio Grande as a disciplinarian with a posi-
tive effect upon the faculty. His preaching there was described as
forceful, tender, and sympathetic.[79] Dunn secured the charter and
bylaws and organized the Board of Trustees in November 1875.
He supervised the construction of a dormitory and dining hall, and
even agreed to serve as president for a short time. The college was
dedicated in August 1876, and Dunn gave the dedication sermon
and prayer. He proceeded then to establish an endowment, and the
school opened to students in September 1876.

In 1876 Dunn visited the churches of freedmen in southern
Illinois. He also took his family to the Centennial Exposition at
Philadelphia. His believed that although he could give his family
few material goods, they would never forget this trip together.

Returning to Hillsdale, Dunn continued to be in demand to
speak at the dedications of new churches. He attracted large audiences at such occasions and raised hundreds of dollars to help pay
building costs. The *Hillsdale Herald* reported on Dunn's dedication
of a church in Orange, Michigan, in 1880: "Not only did he have a
good text (2 Sam 1:1–3), but it was sound on the money question,
a round $800 being raised to pay the entire floating debt upon
the church property before the service closed."[80] Several days later,
Dunn dedicated the Howard City Freewill Baptist Church, where

he raised most of the entire $500 debt that had been incurred during construction.[81]

He was also in demand to deliver funeral orations. He filled the pulpit in neighboring towns, and led the students' weekly prayer meetings on Tuesday evenings. These duties were in addition to his heavy teaching schedule. Perhaps the function most valued by Dunn was to ordain his former students into the ministry. Such young men felt it a great privilege to be endorsed by their mentor.

Dunn maintained a high interest in student events and activities, such as the national championships of Hillsdale's rowing team and the campus literary societies. He spoke to the Amphictyon Society in the spring of 1879. The literary societies were staples of Hillsdale College, he said: "Power in society depends upon two things, symmetry and force. Knowledge is to the mind what food is to the body, and it is just as necessary that it should be digested. Mere knowledge never made a man." He continued: "One of the greatest defects of our educational system is want of symmetrical development. Symmetry is one thing, but there must be motive power back of it. These literary societies by the friction of mind with mind develop this motive power. Cut off these literary societies, and you cut off one-half of that which makes the man."[82]

Ransom and Cyrena Dunn opened their home on occasion to students and professors, holding parties such as one described by the newspaper in military terms: "The company being large, it was invited in two battalions. We can vouch to the fact that the regiments marched up to the attack on the 'goodies' with a bravery that was praiseworthy. Mrs. Dunn's parties are never pinched, either in attendance, enjoyment, or the so-called 'substantials.'"[83]

One Friday evening, Dunn volunteered to be quizzed by students at a round of "live topics" sponsored by the campus Christian Association. Students wrote their questions on slips of paper and deposited them in a box; Dunn fielded over sixty of them. "The Prof., as usual, was equal to the occasion," reported the *Hillsdale Herald*, "and hurled back answers that convinced all that he is a peripatetic encyclopedia."[84]

Dunn proved not so adept at negotiating the stairs to the *Hillsdale Standard* office. Misstepping at the top and falling to the bottom, he dislocated his wrist and fractured his right radius in the autumn of 1878.[85] His colleagues supposed that he would take time out from his heavy schedule and rest a while, but Dunn refused. To keep up his large correspondence, he learned to write with his left hand. And as usual, he prepared and gave lectures daily. The *Hillsdale Herald* reported in November: "If some of our boys, who complain of over-work on three lessons, want an illustration of what a man can do and make no fuss about it either, they have it close at home. Professor Dunn the past term has delivered two class-room lectures a day, preached twenty-six public discourses and two dedication sermons, delivered thirteen lyceum lectures in four different states on different subjects, and half the time he had a broken arm. Break your arms gentlemen, ride a few thousand miles a term, and you will then find time to get your lessons."[86]

A trustee described Dunn at sixty years of age: "It must have been Professor Dunn's constant work that kept him young in spirit as well as vigorous in mind and body. Surely no one could have been freer from the danger of rusting out." Dunn remained quick and energetic. A visitor to one of his classes wrote: "It was my privilege for the first time to listen to the class exercises under Ransom Dunn, with which I was more than pleased. The clear-cut crystallized thoughts uttered by Dr. Dunn, and his peculiarly terse way of putting things, left no excuse for misapprehension on the part of any of the class."[87] He was, as one alumnus described him, "silver-tongued and impetuous."[88]

In an evaluation of theological training in the state, an authority claimed that even the University of Michigan did not surpass the standards of Hillsdale College, as directed by Dunn.[89]

It was fitting that Dunn should deliver a speech titled "Honesty as the Best Policy" at the 1879 Hillsdale County Fair.[90] He began on a humorous note: "Fairs like other enterprises are progressive. To native stock and domestic work was added short horns, Polands, China Pigs and Shanghie Chickens. And now, Profs." He went on to explain the importance of just weights and measures. Awards, he said, should be based on the quality of the work, whether it is the sound of music or the content of a college lecture.[91]

In 1880, Dunn preached at the Centennial Freewill Baptist Conference at Weirs, New Hampshire. The report of the meeting stated that "Professor Dunn probably preached the ablest sermon of his life. It lent dignity to the whole denomination, and will long live in gracious memory."[92] H. M. Ford, a Hillsdale alumnus of the previous year, said that of the leaders of the Freewill Baptist Church, "the highest seat is given to Ransom Dunn in all that glorious company."[93]

Dunn was convinced of the link between reason and faith, and he set out to make the case for a synthesis. Speaking to a YMCA audience on "The Religion of Common Sense," Dunn in January of 1881 argued that "common sense" was conducive to Christian faith. Throughout history, mankind has sought religious devotion, and in the midst of difficulty and disease the search for eternal truths is amplified. Thus it is "human nature to worship," he said. Men find in the religion of common sense some answer to the problem of sin, an answer that must transcend health and even education. Correspondingly, a sense of eternity—of heaven and hell—must set the mentality of daily living.[94]

While continuing his work at Hillsdale—where his classes in theology were the largest ever seen at the College—Dunn meanwhile continued to preach throughout the nation. He occupied the pulpit of the Union Square Church in San Francisco several times. When he spoke at the San Bernardino Congregational Church in Southern California, residents of Riverside fifteen miles away flocked to hear him, and the Riverside newspaper reported: "Professor Dunn is one of the most eloquent pulpit orators in the United States, and the treat was a rare one, never before enjoyed by the people of this valley."[95] Dunn also spoke at a memorial service for his former student, President James Garfield.

In 1883 Dunn decided to resign his place at Hillsdale College in hopes that he might build up denominational interests in the far West. At a retirement service in the Chapel on June 21, the faculty and student body presented Dunn with a ten-volume set of McClintock and Strong's *Religious Encyclopedia*. On behalf of the Board of Trustees, the Honorable J. C. Patterson recounted Dunn's indispensable work for the college and presented him with a purse of $155. When Dunn rose to make his response, the high honors being paid him nearly overwhelmed his emotions. As the *Hillsdale Herald* reported, "Many a manly eye moistened, and an occasional sob told of the deep affection of all for him."[96]

Dunn spent the next year in Nebraska. But pressure was soon brought to bear upon him to return to Hillsdale. President Durgin had resigned to invest his efforts elsewhere, and the trustees urged Dunn to come back. In June 1884, they asked him to supervise the work of raising the endowment. As reported in the newspaper: "No better selection could have been made. If prevailed upon to enter the field, he can do more to secure funds and keep open the channels of acquaintance and sympathy between the public and the college than any other man."[97] When it became clear that Dunn would return from Nebraska, the *Kalamazoo Telegraph* published a warning to its readers: "Look out for Prof. Dunn, of Neb., who will be perambulating the State soon. He is a ministerial looking chap, very magnetic, however, and wonderfully persuasive, telling his story so smoothly that almost unconsciously you will be led into giving your note for a good round sum, or thoughtlessly hand over your pocketbook to him, in the interest of the Hillsdale College endowment fund."[98] The endowment goal: $100,000.[99]

★ ★ ★

Chapter Six

DUNN AT THE HELM

✲ ✲ ✲

THE PRUDENTIAL COMMITTEE of the Board of Trustees resolved on December 9, 1884, to "invite the senior professor,
Rev. Ransom Dunn, to take charge of classes after January 1, 1885,
and to serve as acting president . . . at a salary of $1200/year."[100]
He consented to accept the new responsibilities, but for only two
years. "Speaking of the election of Prof. Dunn to the presidency
of the college," opined the *Hillsdale Business*, "everybody wonders
what the trustees were thinking about, that it was not done twenty
years ago."[101]

After obtaining evidence of misbehavior by two members of
the Sigma Chi fraternity in rooms in the Flatiron Block downtown,
Dunn deactivated the chapter in June 1886. He also maintained
traditions such as women using one stairway in Central Hall and
men the other. Dunn reacted mildly to the student prank of lifting
the president's buggy to the top of Central Tower in 1884, but a
year later he forced other students to stand during his class until
culprits returned the chairs they had stolen from his room.

Tuition at Hillsdale in the 1880s was virtually free due to the increase in endowment. Students contributed at most one-quarter of all institutional income. A student's total cost (board, lodging, fees, and books) for a full year was about $100, the lowest in the state. In one year alone Dunn added $10,000 to the permanent endowment. The treasurer announced a surplus of $2,460.01. The physical appearance of the College grounds had never been in such fine condition. Among the most exciting events of Dunn's presidency was the opening of the Dickerson Gymnasium, the first college gymnasium in Michigan. As with all College buildings, he offered the prayer of dedication at the laying of the cornerstone.

Dunn frequently led evening prayer meeting, considering it the most important activity of the week on campus. "Talk of religious influence," he said one day at the prayer meeting, "this hour, this single hour, once a week, does more to influence character in this college than any ten hours beside." "Who can afford to skip it?" asked the *Hillsdale Herald*.[102] A student wrote in 1883, "Went to prayer meeting in eve. Between 6 and 7. Led by Prof. Dunn. Very earnest and enthusiastic and well attended."[103]

The largest baccalaureate audience in Hillsdale history heard President Dunn's sermon to the graduating class of 1885. One report maintained, "It is only commonplace to say that for more than a quarter of a century Professor Dunn has been the idol of hundreds of the students, but for the first time in college history this teacher, whose thirty years of brilliant service dwarfs the record of all other servants of the college, gives the baccalaureate and presides at commencement as president."[104]

Dunn's subject on this occasion was "Relations of Christianity to Civilization." The Western heritage, he pointed out, was rooted not only in the Christian faith but also in the classical tradition. The civilization this heritage animates is old, and its foundations proven." [T]here are facts in history and experience, principles in sociology and morals which cannot be discarded nor omitted in civilization," he said.

> The light of other ages must be retained though shining in modern lamps. The literature of Greece and the laws of Rome are as real and vital today as in former ages. Christianity involves truths as old and unchanging as the Deity. It looks back upon all the good of the past in appreciative judgment, inquiring "for the old paths." "Where is the good way?" It carefully preserves in history, in doctrines and in its laws, all that is good. Such conservatism is essential to civilization.[105]

But change and progress are also important, he continued. The new life of faith, in its invigoration of civilization, "promotes the fine arts, scientific investigations, discoveries and inventions, schools and liberal governments." He went on: "The gospel assumes the common worth and equality of men in its provisions, promises and laws, recognizing personal responsibility and privileges and social claims and authority."[106]

Dunn told his audience that the capacity both to lead and to follow must guide the character of a self-governing society. "It is natural for every man, under some circumstances, to command, and under other circumstances to obey, and by this duality in human nature do we know that man was made for government—to rule, and to be ruled." And a free people must owe its highest obedience to the moral law of God, for "without moral principle and integrity, civilization cannot be maintained." Character as well as knowledge is indispensable to the preservation of civilization. "Intelligence and conscientiousness must be united in all healthy society and national life."[107]

Thus was the work of education as carried out at Hillsdale
College invaluable, Dunn concluded. Patrick Henry and Abraham
Lincoln, as self-taught men, stood among few exceptions to the
necessity of formal learning.

> We cannot diminish one effort, or afford to merely con-
> tinue as we are. The wants and demands of the world
> and its civilization, of the church and its ministry, of
> the thousands of students in the past and in the future,
> imperatively demand an increase of endowment and
> effort, of faith and sacrifice beyond anything yet attempt-
> ed. God and humanity require it. My dear friends of the
> senior class who leave us with so many, pleasant and
> affecting recollections, whose faithfulness and success
> inspire so many hopes for your future, in this discourse
> is presented your life work. It is not the gratification of
> appetite, pride or ambition, but to civilize the world. Not
> for self, but for the world, yourselves included; rightness
> more than policy, benevolence more than selfishness,
> God more than man, eternity more than time.[108]

Hillsdale College was a fixture with its founder at the helm,
and it was no time to forget either its promise to future generations
or its proud legacy. Ransom Dunn was the embodiment. Beginning
on May 6, 1885, Dunn wrote "The Story of the Planting," an excel-
lent serial sketch of Hillsdale College, which was published in the
first ten issues of *The Reunion*. In it he also argued that Hillsdale
accomplished more in providing sound education and moral standards, in proportion to its means, than other schools.

In 1886, the College secured George F. Mosher, former United
States consul to France and Germany, to take on the duties of president. Dunn accordingly was able to give up his temporary office and

return to the classroom. Most of his time was spent teaching in the Theological Department. Because he was one of only two professors in the department—at that time the only such department in the state—he was overworked. The college catalog specified that "those in good standing, of any denomination, and giving evidence of a call to the ministry, may be admitted to the Theological Course without charge for tuition."

Dunn would begin his course on systematic theology with an explanation of its importance, asserting that there had never been a "successful government but is founded on the principles, the laws of God."[109] The best of art, architecture, and literature was the inspiration of theology. There were three sources of theological knowledge, he taught: intuition, reason, and revelation. He defined reason simply: "We know that certain things are so and that other things are thus; we draw our conclusions so and so is thus and so; and therefore!"[110]

Dunn's second lecture in the course was entitled "Atheism." Atheistic beliefs could be divided into Materialism, Pantheism, and Agnosticism. Dunn found atheism to be the unbelievable thing; God, he thought, is rather evident to man. "Is it true that we cannot know there is a God?" he asked his class in 1886. Knowing God if only by natural revelation was to view Him as the Creator. Evolution, to Dunn, was as false as atheism. "There is no evidence of change of species nor of organic life from inorganic life. A species may be improved and made better, as for instance the horse and the dog. But the dog will never become a horse; the species are not changed. Nor can we find in all our research and study that from inorganic things, from the rock for instance, organic life has ever been brought forth."[111]

Atheism, "anarchy and sensuality," the opposites of theistic developments—"civilization, Art, Science, Government." Atheism led to relativism; it deluded the conscience. "All good in the world depends upon the sense of right and wrong," Dunn told his students. "It is an awful state of things to be without a sense of right and wrong."[112]

Dunn's personal magnetism and the example of his daily life most impressed his students. One graduate wrote, "My most helpful memories of college are of my esteemed, revered, and much loved teacher and friend, Professor Dunn, who put his whole soul into helping his pupils to be patient, persevering, sympathetic, diligent, orderly, kind, and cheerful, and to have in store a fund of common sense for life's work."[113]

In 1886, Dunn's daughter Nettie (born in 1863) became National Secretary of the YWCA. Upon graduation from Hillsdale, Nettie had become lady principal of Rio Grande College in Ohio, and in 1880 she had been appointed as a visiting instructor in Latin and Literature at Hillsdale.[114] As YWCA Secretary, she traveled the country calling young ladies to the mission field.[115]

Ransom Dunn took time to do missionary work in Florida and Georgia, attending churches with large black congregations. He was dismayed by continuing conflicts between the races, although there were signs of improvement. He also was distressed to find so much poverty in the rural South.

Dunn frequently was asked to compile a volume of his theological lectures. During 1889–1890, he devoted all the time he could spare to preparing a series of lectures titled *Systematic Theology*. The 467-page manuscript was sent to a publisher in the spring of 1890. Of practical use to ministers, the book was of equal interest to the general reader. Dunn had another manuscript, "Practical Theology," also ready for the printer.

Continuing the work of the College, Dunn believed, would require new efficiency of resource allocation. He published an article in 1887 alleging that a "scatteration" problem had developed within the Freewill Baptist denomination, and that new priorities had to be established to secure the future of its institutions.[116] In 1889 he addressed the Hillsdale College Alumni Association on the need for alumni support: "We live in the past and in the future, and of that future let me prophesy: From this body of men and women and their successors shall come the benefactors who shall make Hillsdale College great and eternal."[117]

His health continued to hold up. He wrote in 1890, "I rode in mud and rain twenty miles in a buggy and preached twice yesterday and am quite comfortable today."[118] At 75 years of age, his resilience was remarkable. And he never abandoned raising college endowment. One donor wrote, "It seems to me the college will not be Hillsdale College without him."[119] In 1892 he attended the centennial of the New Hampshire Freewill Baptist Yearly Meeting at New Durham, where he preached to a crowd of 1,500 in a large tent. The official report stated that "this venerable educator, whose name is a household word among all our Israel, came to the front. . . . The treatment, the style, the enthusiasm, were characteristic of the man and worthy of the occasion."[120]

In 1894, Dunn gave an all-College lecture in the chapel titled "The History of the College." As he wrote at the close of the college year that June, "For the last six weeks I have averaged three hundred miles a week and more than two sermons a Sabbath. Last Sabbath I spent in Canada . . . and the following week an ordination north of Lansing."[121] In early 1895 he wrote, "I am well, of course, for I have attended seven funerals in three weeks and a wedding, with my daily class work and supplying regularly the Baptist pulpit in the city."[122] On June 20, 1895, Dunn gave the invocation at the dedication of the Alpha Kappa Phi Civil War monument by the renowned sculptor Lorado Taft, which is located on the front campus.[123]

On May 20, 1896, his wife Cyrena died. She suffered from rheumatism and neurological ailments, though while wintering in Los Angeles earlier that year her health had seemed to improve. Upon their return to Hillsdale in the spring, however, she took a bad turn. When a doctor was called to her bedside, she told him, "Doctor, I have come to die." Her husband was by her side when the end came.

The funeral was held the following Saturday at College Baptist Church. College activities were suspended for the morning and the church was filled. President Mosher noted the inseparable bond between the Dunns; a friend, Mrs. Copp, spoke about Cyrena's devotion to the home life and success of her husband. C. H. Gurney eulogized Cyrena Dunn as "a woman who lived for others." She was a quiet and graceful servant to her family and church whose "influence on College Hill will last as long as there is social life, a Free Baptist Church and a Hillsdale College."

The entire Hillsdale College community joined with Dunn in mourning. As the *Hillsdale Herald* wrote, "His long, loving, and untiring service in connection with the college, his upright and Christian principles as a man, have endeared him to thousands whose hearts beat with the most tender sympathy for him in his sad hour of affliction from the loss of his beloved wife."[124]

✯ ✯ ✯

Chapter Seven

DEATH AND LEGACY

★ ★ ★

IN A QUIET MOSSY ROW of Oak Grove Cemetery north of Hillsdale's campus sit seven markers belonging to the Dunn family. Six of the seven were set in place before the one marked "Father." Carved on the central headstone are these words: "Together they labored here. They rest together there. Forever with the Lord."

Dunn would frequently walk through Oak Grove Cemetery, sad pilgrimages for the lonely old man. He had lost both parents, nine brothers and sisters, two wives, five children, and many dear friends. Yet Ransom Dunn never allowed the loss of a loved one to end his goals of service to others. Though slowed by age and sorrow, he continued to be the living symbol of an institution.

"The venerable form of Dr. Dunn, as seen upon the streets since his great bereavement, moves slower and is more bowed down than usual, but his mind does not impair by age nor sorrow, and his heart beats as warmly to every interest of the college as ever," reported the *Hillsdale Herald*.[125] Eighty percent of the American colleges founded before the Civil War had failed, while Hillsdale flourished. Dunn maintained that he had much reason for thanksgiving, and he continued to pray, "My Lord, thy will be done."

Dunn's greatest satisfaction, as always, continued to come from teaching. He wrote at the beginning of a new semester, "I feel more natural in the classroom than anywhere else."[126] His academic standards in the Theological Department remained high, and half of the students failed his examination in one class. In addition to classes and to his usual speechmaking events, he also took time to lecture at the Law Department of the University of Michigan.

In 1896, the first Hillsdale yearbook, *The Wolverine*, was dedicated to Ransom Dunn. It contained his essay "Financial Values of Hillsdale College." "The real value of colleges and universities," he wrote in it, "is not to be estimated by the millions invested in their endowments . . . but by the increase of mental power and moral force."

During his long career, Dunn had taught a total of thirteen subjects. Recognized for his dedication to teaching for over four decades, he had also been Hillsdale's chief fundraiser, served as interim president, and been a trustee from 1855 until his death. It is no wonder that he received the title "The Grand Old Man of Hillsdale."

Five of Dunn's children and nine of his grandchildren graduated from Hillsdale College. On the lecture circuit at Ocean Park, Maine, the poet Will Carleton once remarked, after an introduction by his old Professor Dunn, that Ransom Dunn was the only man still working at Hillsdale College who had been there when Carleton was a student during the Civil War.[127]

As Dunn neared retirement, he received the first of numerous honors. At the 1897 commencement exercises, he was presented

with a gold-headed cane, a gift from faculty, students, and friends.
A poem written for the occasion contained the following verse:

> Titles such as kings could give him
> Could but mar his Maker's plan
> And the name that best befits him
> Is the simple "Grand Old Man."

Dunn was now 80 years of age. Friends presented him with
a volume of letters. A document sent by three college officials contained this quotation from Henry Wadsworth Longfellow: "I shall
pass through this world but once; any good thing, therefore, that I
can do or any kindness that I can show, let me do it now. Let me not
defer it nor neglect it, for I shall not pass this way again."[128]

Because of declining health, Dunn decided to close his college
work on June 13, 1898. In his resignation letter to the trustees he
wrote, "I hope to be remembered as a friend of Christian enterprise."
A committee of the trustees responded, "To Dunn's energy and
enthusiasm in its early days are due its origin and growth more than
to any other man." After raising the college's founding endowment
in the 1850s, he would secure $74,000 in special pledges, $5,900
in notes, and $1,900 in cash. This made a total of over $104,000
that he added to the college endowment.

On July 22, 1898, John Wolford wrote to Dunn about his student days in the 1870s: "May the twilight of your life be as peaceful
and happy as your manhood's life has been noble and grand in the
uplifting and upbuilding of your fellow man, and I know this to be
the voice and sentiment of every boy and girl that have matriculated
in old Hillsdale College."[129]

Dunn continued to speak at conventions, such as the General
Freewill Baptist Conference at Ocean Park. There he made new

friends, one of whom later commented, "His was a strong, helpful life; it was a privilege to have known him if only for a short
time."

Dunn's final trip to Hillsdale was for Commencement in 1900.
The alumni banquet was held in the College chapel, and Dunn was
called upon for the first toast. A rousing ovation delayed his speech,
his last message to the alumni. At his final trustees' meeting, he
calmly pointed out a serious weakness in one of the proposals, and
the motion was promptly withdrawn. Dunn also continued fundraising during his last years: Traveling to Nebraska at one point, he
returned with a deed for 160 acres worth $800.

Dunn's last months were spent at the home of his daughter,
Mrs. Helen Dunn Gates, in Scranton, Pennsylvania, where he continued to write articles. One editor said that "his last copy, written
the week that he died, was clear and distinct and free from error
as on previous occasions." He passed away on November 9, 1900,
at the age of 82 years, falling from his chair at the dining table and
passing within a minute.

After brief services at Scranton, Ransom Dunn's body was
returned to his Hillsdale home. On November 11, 1900, a proces-
sion of students and faculty marched from Central Hall to the Dunn
home on Hillsdale Street. Family and friends in carriages followed
the hearse to the College Baptist Church, led by the honor escort
of the student body. All businesses in the city were closed.

Professor C. H. Gurney spoke for faculty and students: "His
faith in Hillsdale College and its future was a thing sublime. That
faith gave courage to many other hearts. When others thought pos-
sibly evil influences and machinations might eventually succeed, his
confidence was unshaken, and he saw the right triumph. . . . It may
truthfully and modestly be said that no one ever lived in Hillsdale who
was accorded a higher degree of respect and honor than he."[130]

L. A. Crandall spoke for the College alumni: "There are no money measurements for the gift which this man made to Hillsdale and so to humanity. He gave his lifeblood. All that he had, all that he was, all that he could accomplish, he gave with joy to us. . . . But he still lives, aye, and shall continue to live down the centuries, in this institution which he served with such matchless devotion and in the lives which he inspired and shaped."[131]

Another tribute to Dunn stated, "If all the schools that Dr. Dunn helped to establish should perish, if all the churches he organized should be dissolved, if the denomination itself for which he labored so long should lose its identity, still his monument would remain in the lasting influence of his personality in individual lives." Many other letters contained the same idea.

Ransom Dunn had accomplished much as a minister by writing and preaching, and he had dedicated more than one hundred churches. Most of all, he had been a founder of American education. He had shaped the basic characteristics of Hillsdale College, including emphasis upon independence. As a newspaper reported in 1888, "It is this stern self-reliant spirit, born of self denial and persevering effort, that makes Hillsdale's sons and daughters so marvelously successful in their broader after life. Of its moral and religious influences too much cannot be said."[132] And it was due largely to Dunn's fundraising and emphasis on efficiency that as late as 1899 student fees amounted to only $19 a year.[133]

President Joseph Mauck wrote in 1924:

Professor Dunn brought to the College a great deal more than has been or can be definitely "credited" to him. Undoubtedly, for example, his sermons, lectures, funeral and wedding services, and the like, so aroused the philanthropic sentiments that money was afterward given or bequeathed and the giver did not so much as consider who gave him the first inspiration. . . . He cannot be measured by dollars, but by the cold standard that Hillsdale College would hardly be here now but for what he "raised." We recognize in him a man of eminent ability and character, and one whose devotion and loyalty to the college have ever been singularly heroic. In short, it is difficult to find words adequate to express the love and esteem in which we hold him.[134]

Our Journal of Keuka College in New York wrote of Dunn's "long life full of hard, successful work. He was a great revivalist, and hundreds were saved through his preaching. He was a leader with Hale, Whittier, and others in the antislavery reform, and a constant temperance agitator. For over forty years he was a professor in the theological school at Hillsdale, and did more for that institution, perhaps, than any other man. He was a scholar, in spite of weak eyes that forbade much study when young, for he studied all his life. He was a prodigious worker, though he carried ever a frail body. . . ."[135] Will Carleton's *Everywhere* claimed that Dunn was "one of the most brilliant pulpit orators that our country has produced."[136]

Carleton, a Hillsdale graduate, wrote of his alma mater:

> So shall we work for high Heaven and further
>   our Maker's intention;
> For though man must run the machinery,
>   The college is God's own invention.

Hillsdale's *Standard* wrote, "His active work was largely done in the West, doing pioneer work for Christianity in Ohio, Wisconsin and Indiana, as well as Michigan. It is as one of the founders of the college here, however, that his name will ever be inseparably connected. For nearly fifty years Dr. Dunn has labored and prayed for Hillsdale College; through all its successes and vicissitudes he has stood faithful, helpful, and inspiring. . . . Hillsdale College may well say of Dr. Dunn:'He was a man, take him for all and all / We shall not look upon his like again.'"[137]

The Collegian, the student publication of Hillsdale College, stated, "No title was ever more deserved than that of 'The Father of Hillsdale College.' From the day he looked about him in the wilderness which then spread over College Hill and said, "We will have a college here" to the hour he breathed his last on Friday, Hillsdale, her present welfare and her outlook for the future, have always been dear to his heart."[138] As Hillsdale's founder, Dunn, more than anyone, insisted from its beginning that the College be consistent with "moral and social instruction as will best develop the minds and improve the hearts of the pupils."[139]

Joseph W. Mauck, alumnus and future president of Hillsdale College, had written to Dunn in 1886: "On the ground before the college was founded, continuously a trustee for 36 years . . . always an elder brother, a father in spirit to us all as students, with a remarkably small number of mistakes in a long and leading career . . . you have justly gained and held the love and confidence of the thousands who have entered the college."[140]

Dunn had left his New England home as a "boy preacher" at the age of 18. His close acquaintances included John Greenleaf Whittier, Charles Sumner, William Lloyd Garrison, Henry Ward Beecher, Edward Everett, Joshua R. Giddings, John P. Hale, and Benjamin Wade. Yet Dunn abandoned the relative comforts of the East to accept the hardships and challenges of the Michigan frontier.

President George F. Mosher, attending a denominational gathering in Iowa and not able to be at Dunn's funeral, sent this message: "He was a good man. May his death ring out a new call for the same heroic, devoted, cheerful service as that which characterized the more than sixty years of his restless life."[141] In July of 1918, the College observed the centenary of Dunn's birth with suitable tributes delivered at the College Church.

★ ★ ★

Today, on a still spring morning as the birds sing their chorus from the oak trees, Hillsdale College comes alive. A professor strolls into Delp Hall to grade midterm exams before convening his seminar on Western Heritage. Students, hopeful and ambitious, discuss Aristotle's *Politics*, the Book of Job, and the works of C. S. Lewis beside Lorado Taft's Civil War statue. From the Howard Music Building strains of jazz float through open windows to the ears of a sorority member leaving her house for a biology class. Past the Sports Complex and the football field, the day is beginning at Hillsdale Academy as K-12 students recite the Pledge of Allegiance around the flagpole. And in the middle of it all rings the bell atop Central Hall.

To millions of Americans, Central Hall is a symbol of Hillsdale's principles. These principles are old and enduring.

Within the cornerstone of Central Hall is the prayer of Ransom Dunn: "May earth be better and heaven be richer because of the life and labor of Hillsdale College." It was what the Apostle might have called "the effective, fervent prayer of a righteous man." Ransom Dunn lived to see his prayer answered, and the answer echoes through the ages. It is in our own age—busy, uncertain of meaning, beset by the degradations of postmodernity—that Ransom Dunn's prayer is as vibrant and important as ever. Hillsdale today is much like the Hillsdale Dunn knew—independent, faithful, patriotic, small and yet great, still dedicated to its original mission.

Hillsdale College sometimes seems to fight a lonely battle. But it would be forgetting its roots to despair. Now and then, in the midst of a raging January snowstorm through the rolling hills of southern Michigan, when the sounds and speeds of the world around are muted and time seems paused, one can almost see the ghost of a tall old man riding alone on horseback into Hillsdale. He rides with confidence. He will not leave until his work is finished.

✳ ✳ ✳

NOTES

[1]Much of the information in this book is taken from Helen Dunn Gates, *A Sketch of the Life and Labors of Rev. Ransom Dunn, D.D.* (Boston: The Morningstar Publishing House, 1901). The book has been long out of print.

[2]Ibid., p. 17.

[3]*Hillsdale Herald*, November 25, 1886.

[4]Gates, *Life and Labors*, p. 26.

[5]Ibid., pp. 27–28.

[6]Alexis de Tocqueville, *Democracy in America*, ed. Harvey C. Mansfield and Delba Winthrop (Chicago: University of Chicago Press, 2000), p. 281.

[7]Gates, *Life and Labors*, p. 36.

[8]*The Collegian-Herald* [Hillsdale College], August 18, 1898.

[9]Bulletin of First Freewill Baptist Church, Jonesboro, Arkansas.

[10]*Hillsdale Herald*, June 10, 1880.

[11]John R. McKivigan, *The War against Proslavery Religion* (Ithaca: Cornell University Press, 1984), p. 28.

[12]Gates, *Life and Labors of Ransom Dunn*, pp. 71–72.

[13]Ibid., pp. 70–71.

[14]Ibid., p. 72.

[15]Ibid., p. 89.

¹⁶Ransom Dunn, "A Discourse on the Freedom of the Will," March 1, 1850.

¹⁷Ibid.

¹⁸Ibid.

¹⁹Gates, *Life and Labors*, p. 97.

²⁰Timothy L. Smith, *Revivalism and Social Reform* (Gloucester, MA: Peter Smith, 1976), p. 26.

²¹See Edwin Gaustad, *Historical Atlas of Religion in America* (New York: Harper & Row, 1976).

²²Donald Tewksbury, *The Founding of American Colleges and Universities before the Civil War* (New York: Teachers College Press, 1932), p. 111.

²³Ibid., p. 117.

²⁴Free Baptist Church Covenant of Hillsdale College, gift of Mrs. Jewel Pfeifer Estes.

²⁵Edmund Fairfield to Ransom Dunn, November 20, 1848, Ransom Dunn papers, Bentley Historical Library, University of Michigan, Ann Arbor.

²⁶Edmund Fairfield to Ransom Dunn, November 22, 1848, Ransom Dunn papers, Bentley Historical Library, University of Michigan, Ann Arbor.

²⁷Edmund Fairfield to Ransom Dunn, December 22, 1851, Ransom Dunn papers, Bentley Historical Library, University of Michigan, Ann Arbor.

²⁸Gates, *Life and Labors*, pp. 108–9.

²⁹William Terman, *Spring Arbor Township, 1830–1980* (Spring Arbor, MI: 1977), p. 243.

³⁰Arlan K. Gilbert, *Historic Hillsdale College: Pioneer in Higher Education, 1844–1900* (Hillsdale, MI: Hillsdale College Press, 1991), p. 27.

³¹D. M. Fisk, "The Story of the Planting," *The Reunion*, May 6, 1885.

³²John C. Patterson, "History of Hillsdale College," 1883 article reprinted in *Collection of the Pioneer Society of the State of Michigan*, VI (Lansing, MI: State Printers, 1907), p. 149.

³³Ibid.

³⁴David B. Potts, "Baptist Colleges in the Development of American Society, 1812–1861," Ph.D. thesis, Harvard University, 1967, p. 153.

[35]Michigan Southern Railroad, Chicago Historical Society.

[36]See Potts, "Baptist Colleges in the Development of American Society."

[37]Edmund Fairfield to Ransom Dunn, January 26, 1853, Ransom Dunn papers, Bentley Historical Library, University of Michigan, Ann Arbor.

[38]*The American Citizen*, February 2, 1853.

[39]Fisk, "The Story of the Planting."

[40]Gates, *Life and Labors*, p. 114.

[41]Dr. D. D. Ball, "Our Colleges," in *Hillsdale Herald*, November 17, 1887.

[42]Fisk, "The Story of the Planting."

[43]Potts, *Baptist Colleges*, p. 215.

[44]Ransom Dunn papers, Bentley Historical Library, University of Michigan, Ann Arbor.

[45]Ibid.

[46]Gates, *Life and Labors*, p. 130.

[47]Ibid., p. 134.

[48]Ibid., p. 137.

[49]Harry J. Brown and Frederick D. Williams, eds., *The Diary of James A. Garfield* (East Lansing, MI: Michigan State University Press, 1967) I, 14; Hendrik Booraem, *James A. Garfield and His World, 1844–1852* (Lewisburg, PA: Bucknell University Press, 1988), V, p. 99.

[50]*Hillsdale Herald*, June 18, 1880.

[51]*Advance*, January 13, 1886.

[52]Gates, *Life and Labors*, p. 150.

[53]*Hillsdale Herald*, June 7, 1883.

[54]Gates, *Life and Labors*, p. 123.

[55]Roy Basler, ed., *The Collected Works of Abraham Lincoln* (New Brunswick, NJ: Rutgers University Press, 1953), VI, pp. 545–46.

[56]*Hillsdale Standard*, June 23, 1885.

[57]Newell Ransom Dunn to his father, September 26, 1862. Newell Ransom Dunn Collection, Bentley Historical Library, University of Michigan, Ann Arbor.

[58]Wayland Dunn Collection, Bentley Historical Library, University of Michigan, Ann Arbor.

[59]Wayland Dunn to father, November 25, 1863, Bentley Historical Library, University of Michigan, Ann Arbor.

[60]Captain Joseph McKnight to Ransom Dunn, February 23, 1863. Ransom Dunn Collection, Bentley Historical Library, University of Michigan, Ann Arbor.

[61]Ibid., Newell Ransom Dunn to his father, October 18, 1862.

[62]Wayland Dunn to his father, March 28, 1863. Francis Wayland Dunn Collection, Bentley Historical Library, University of Michigan, Ann Arbor.

[63]Ibid.

[64]Ibid., Ransom Dunn to Wayland Dunn, April 2, 1863.

[65]Arlan K. Gilbert, *Hillsdale Honor: The Civil War Experience* (Hillsdale, MI: Hillsdale College Press, 1994), p. 72.

[66]Gates, *Life and Labors*, p. 157.

[67]Captain Jacob H. Stark to Professor Dunn, March 21, 1865. Ransom Dunn Collection, Bentley Historical Library, University of Michigan, Ann Arbor.

[68]Chaplain N. Woodworth to Ransom Dunn, November 2, 1864. Ransom Dunn Collection, Bentley Historical Library, University of Michigan, Ann Arbor.

[69]Wayland Dunn diaries, July 23, 1864, Bentley Historical Library, University of Michigan, Ann Arbor.

[70]Document from the Ransom Dunn Collection, Bentley Historical Library, University of Michigan, Ann Arbor.

[71]Ben. Cottrino to Ransom Dunn, Troy Grove, October 13, 1861. Ransom Dunn Collection, Bentley Historical Library, University of Michigan, Ann Arbor.

[72]Wayland Dunn to his father, August 25, 1864. Bentley Historical Library, University of Michigan, Ann Arbor.

[73]Gates, *Life and Labors*, p. 161.

[74]H. M. Ford, "Some Reminiscences of the College Church and Its Pastors," June 10, 1934.

[75]*Hillsdale Herald*, July 25, 1895.

[76]*Lansing Republican*, December 5, 1872.

[77]Minutes of Hillsdale College Board of Trustees, March 6, 1874.

[78]*Hillsdale Standard*, August 25, 1874.

[79]James S. Porter, *Lamp of the Woods* (Rio Grande, OH: Rio Grande College, 1976), pp. 11–13.

[80]*Hillsdale Herald*, May 20, 1880.

[81]Ibid., June 10, 1880.

[82]Ibid., April 24, 1879.

[83]Ibid., February 12, 1880.

[84]Ibid., December 18, 1884.

[85]Ibid., October 10, 1878.

[86]Ibid., November 28, 1878.

[87]*Hillsdale Standard*, June 5, 1877.

[88]*Hillsdale Herald*, June 18, 1885.

[89]Dr. Richard James in the *Michigan Teacher*, quoted in *Hillsdale Standard*, May 16, 1876.

[90]*Hillsdale Herald*, October 2, 1879.

[91]Ransom Dunn, 1879, Ransom Dunn papers, Bentley Historical Library, University of Michigan, Ann Arbor.

[92]Gates, *Life and Labors*, p. 190.

[93]Ibid., p. 192.

[94]*Hillsdale Herald*, January 6, 1881.

[95]Ibid., September 1, 1881.

[96]Ibid., July 5, 1883.

[97]Ibid., June 19, 1884.

[98]Ibid., July 24, 1884.

[99]Ibid., January 1, 1885.

[100]Ransom Dunn Papers, 1884, Bentley Historical Library, University of Michigan, Ann Arbor.

[101]*Hillsdale Business*, cited in *Hillsdale Herald*, January 15, 1885.

[102]*Hillsdale Herald*, May 27, 1880.

[103]L. E. Dow diary, entry for January 9, 1883, property of Libby Rick.

[104]Gates, *Life and Labors*, p. 205.

[105]Ransom Dunn, "Relations of Christianity to Civilization," *The Reunion*, July 1, 1885.

[106]Ibid.

[107]Ibid.

[108]Ibid.

[109]Frank E. Kenyon, notes on Dunn lectures in "Systematic Theology," 1886, Hillsdale College archives.

[110]Ibid.

[111]Ibid.

[112]Ibid.

[113]Gates, *Life and Labors*, p. 215.

[114]*Hillsdale Herald*, December 9, 1880.

[115]Ibid., March 3, 1887.

[116]Ibid., August 25, 1887.

[117]*Hillsdale Standard*, June 24, 1890.

[118]Gates, *Life and Labors*, p. 223.

[119]Ibid., p. 224.

[120]Ibid., p. 225.

[121]Ibid., p. 228.

[122]Ibid., p. 229.

[123]*Hillsdale Herald*, June 6, 1895.

[124]Ibid., June 3, 1896.

[125]Ibid.

[126]Gates, *Life and Labors*, p. 246.

[127]*Hillsdale Standard*, August 27, 1885.

[128]Gates, *Life and Labors*, pp. 254–55.

[129]John Wolford to Ransom Dunn, July 22, 1898, possession of author.

[130]Gates, *Life and Labors*, pp. 278–79.

[131]Ibid., pp. 283–85.

[132]*Free Baptist*, September 12, 1888.

[133]*Hillsdale Standard*, April 4, 1899.

[134]Mauck to William Slayton, June 16, 1924, Hillsdale College archives.

[135]Gates, *Life and Labors*, pp. 291–92.

[136]As cited in Carleton's paper, "Everywhere." See ibid., p. 292.

[137]*Hillsdale Standard*, November 13, 1900.

[138]Gates, *Life and Labors*, pp. 294–95.

[139]Ibid., April 3, 1855.

[140]J. W. Mauck to Ransom Dunn, August 31, 1886, Ransom Dunn papers, Bentley Historical Library, University of Michigan, Ann Arbor.

[141]Gates, *Life and Labors*, p. 296.

INDEX

ARLAN GILBERT was a member of the History Department at Hillsdale College for 38 years. He served a decade as department chairman, and the seniors elected him Professor of the Year in 1984. He served seven years as senior faculty member at Hillsdale, and his awards include the Alumni Association's honorary alumnus in 1992 and the annual Charger Award for his contributions to athletics. During the College's sesquicentennial, he was presented with an honorary doctor of philosophy degree. He is also a member of Hillsdale's President's Club, which recognizes outstanding supporters of the College. Dr. Gilbert has written three previous books on the history of Hillsdale College. Soon after retiring from teaching, he assumed the position of Hillsdale College Historian.